THE LIGHT OFF CAPE LOOKOUT

ROBERT BENSE

THE LIGHT OFF CAPE LOOKOUT

POEMS

Belle Fontaine Editions

Cover Art: "Troubled Bridges," a painting by Don Jordan. Date unknown. © 2018

Lighthouse Sketch by Bob Miller © 2018

ISBN: 978-0-9965018-9-7

Library of Congress # 2018946304

Published by: Belle Fontaine Editions
509 Hartnell Place
Sacramento, CA 95825

Version: 2018.08.13

This is a privately published and printed book. (The figures and narratives herein are purely imaginary, including the voice in the first person.)

Belle Fontaine Editions

for Laura Melliere Moehrs

(who first brought me to boxwood)

Contents

I

Through a Dark Glass Clearly /3

Memory and Time at the Front of the Mind /4

Geography of Light and Place /6

Profile in Negative Space /8

At Babylon's Far Edge /9

An Evening with the China /10

Casting Wide /11

An Epigraph from Time /12

In the Lost Childhood of Judas... /14

An Inference of Scale /15

Traveling with the Light /16

II

On A Clear Day /21

Solvents of State /22

The Harsh History of Blue /23

Journey to a Funeral /24

Last Dahlia /25

Mentioning the Unmentionable /27

Between Syllables and Sound /28

Transparency /29

Orders of the Prodigal /31

The Lasting of What Matters /33

Composition of Absence /35

III

Catching up with Time /39

As for the Stars /41

Half-past Four /42

Original Intent /43

Mood in a Minor Key /44

How It Seems /45

Cold Queries /46

Measure of Devastation: Part B /48

Latitudes of Grief /49

Horizons /50

Visionary Gestures /51

Where Are the Memories... /53

IV

Personal Geometry /57

The House at Paint Creek /59

Petitioning the Horizon /60

Eclogue /61

Meeting the Chimera Halfway /62

What Things Know /63

Arrival at a Clearing /64

The Domicile of Exile /65

The Nativity at Ames /66

Where Emptiness Settles /67

Canticle for Early Morning /68

V

Trespassing on Time /71

Sailing to the Moon: Tahiti 1947 /73

After This Nothing Happened /75

Not Likely the Last Word /77

A Stiff, Straight-Necked Vase /78

Drift of Delft's Blue and White /79

At Home on the Range /80

Impulses in Counterpoint /81

Nearing Santa Fe /82

Late Fall and a Round /83

In Lost Pursuit /85

Last Train from Blooming Glen /86

VI

Purposiveness without Purpose /91

Unfinished Business /93

Singular Discernments /94

Shorter Cadences /95

Very Likely in France /97

Portrait in Chiaroscuro /98

Regal Indigence /101

When Light Escapes Us /102

Remembering Transience /103

Ventura Vespers /104

Weather in the East Comes from the West /105

I read poetry to save time.

Marilyn Monroe

(Perhaps apocryphal; almost certainly accurate.)

I

Through a Dark Glass Clearly

Those parlors of saxophone bawd
the fogged inland nights
and you look for what's clear
in the subterranean near
the seductive night beam
of e-cigarette ash
chink and clink of glass
in a landscape of haze
—the evenings, like our friends
and us, out on the night
usually end on a note
—the note itself
like the random in chance
(you're lucky or not
some other place, some other day
telling how it would have turned out)
—and looking for what's clear
in the infinite near
you hear the funky backroom jazz
interior lights turned down
and the shadows from your life
turning over in the dark
and looking for light.

Memory and Time
at the Front of the Mind

A hilltop schoolhouse, one room
of numbers, letters in the Palmer Method
then the world's threadbare points of view
new signs of cosmic indifference
falling out of the cosmic order
(doesn't it seem like indifference?)
and whispering alternative passages
to memory and dreams—

imagine cruising old US 66
swerving through Albuquerque
Navaho rugs and chili at Fred Harvey's
two days to gaudy, beguiling LA
and lanterns from receding shores
of the worn coast of the ordinary
waving every which way
to ships of whatever flag
blinded by the inland fog
of the harum-scarum daily
its tornadoes
the hurricanes
a landscape of hazard, surely

and always those other things beyond
us, beyond our bodies
yours and mine—
commanding like a mist over water
and everywhere the immensity
of time's anomie
hardly restrained even by
the rims of radar and palisade
a ragged country and its countryside
now aftermath in the rearview.

Geography of Light and Place

After the formal authority
of boxwood, holly, yew
the strict forms, their long shadows
falling on winter
and throwing all that ends in childhood
into a deep, remembered relief
—and as spectral outlines in snow
feeling their way to the sun's limits
to disappear with time
time itself extended by green borders
running on and on toward the farther on

—sea bones of the vanished
wash up on sand
another age enters
now walking with a hunch
a chair rocking at the railing
interior lights turned down
the dying huddled in their beds
knees fetal bent
each wound
petitioning death, and death whispering
comfort and escape

—a world
(don't they say?) passing away
like the strawberry fields of forever
while drafting a preliminary sketch of us
as in the fugitive history of us
in our forgettable places
to be forgotten again.

Profile in Negative Space

Light dances on the water
at a fountain in the square.
(Yet another day for reflection.)
Columns of public magnificence
overturned in the forum
lie everywhere about.
(Now a landscape of hazard.
Surely the guidebook will say
earthquake and war.)
I wait at a café with time
on my hands. Rest my bad leg
while browsing an old
Herald Tribune. And scan
negative space in the puzzle—
find squarely in front
the hidden countenance
peering out, a sudden
outline of someone I know
from the vast anonymous.
And seeing the face
I recognize the grimace
after so much
(and all the years)
that have come between us.

At Babylon's Far Edge

Not long after those awful times
when fire of the flute had already
singed its reed, Sumerian soldiers
strode past the battered walls
and a glazed Assyrian bull in bas relief
pronged a tortured sky.
Everywhere crazed tile
limned the desert's turquoise horizon
and an old religion's heaven
hovering over a remote landscape
of hazard's gaze.
That was then.
Tumult of war and threadbare
madnesses pushed on through
shoving old dust ahead of new.
This is now.
If you come tomorrow
touring scars ancestors have left
you come too early, if not too late
for the view.

An Evening with the China

Returning from an Eastern sadness
older, thicker, he ambles out from among
the self-absorbed china, descends
in a ceremony of flutter
                                    at the Biedermeier
credenza where some silked in Hèrmes
sip absinthe, other patrons slum
in sackyards and look down
                                    slim noses—
their chins, thighs, tucks once sublime
in time's ornate oval frame, now like a frazzled
Longinus, having lost their highs, their prime

and after an imperial Latin high dive
turning his back on Ovid, some suave
fall leaf paintings, nymphs, the grotto
in a blue-lit cove
                        —it is still a rented world
and at a loss what to recommend for
ennui, insomnia of the long night, those dolors
of the otherwise favored
                                    he remembers
he's no longer secretary for the cabinet's wistful
porcelain and turns nostalgic
for time's earlier, tauter republic.

Casting Wide

The Earth flat
on its back, the world
twisting in pain
the body smell
in those dying fields
the dead huddled in their beds
women grasping their
loss, grieving at graves

you hear the voice of Jesus saying
the animal mourning
of the human heart
reveals nothing
is quite as advertised

so the throw of dice
that odd dispensation of things
seldom shakes out as
something generous
a lovers' blanket shared
or a winter's table set
the crystal and glitter
seeking the full moon
now overlooking shards
of the street's broken glass.

An Epigraph from Time

Here at the beginning of a fresh ending
feeling you have been visiting yourself
and may have overstayed

after the turn taken from happiness
always some evening, a day almost like any

and moving toward the rocks
in the years of a life shared, finding

the unmaking of a house and home

—in time you become
what the young flee from

those winter intimations of oblivion
birds dropping from the sky, the rivers frozen

and following the dilatory fog
sedating a manic city
where the dying lie huddled in their beds

until the western doors open
and you remember
for a while

a harrowed place, forgettable
and to be forgotten again, and then

that someone there has remembered you.

In the Lost Childhood of Judas ...

remembering
Graham Greene and AE

Antics of childhood
the native savageries of youth in its terrible
emptinesses
sometimes start like tryouts—
first for imaginary violent roles, or as prepping
for later torture.

These still require practice.
Schoolyard hazing. The bullying games.
Fraternities. (They would never ax your head?
Your arm—would they?)

But it's too early for perspective.
For the long view of hazardous landscapes
where everything, every idea is heard
through a barrel.

Think of the single idea: cosmic indifference.
If childhood's house
and its attic of memories and regret
are big enough for tomorrow
maybe the cover of diffidence
and drift will suffice to get you through.

An Inference of Scale

Hot-house begonias
the baroque accents of ranunculi
iron-age hydrangeas clinging
to the yard's steep decline
a landscape of hazard
and white winter coming on
herald a pilgrim's winter wonder
and we see what we share
with the greenest gardens
in raw instances of January
the dying huddled in their beds
knees fetal bent
death has become its own
memorial to the monument
of biological moments
and time resists the flower's song
though what lives
may not be what dies
each wound petitioning death
and the difference
offers surcease from nothing
and after hurry
everyone is careful
to mark nothing down.

Traveling with the Light

Light arrives as time
off Cape Lookout
with the hurricanes
the sea lanes passing by
a diurnal logic of rhythm
forcing hands of clocks
—or was it mere space all along
and not the metronomes of time
measuring all that will be taken
from the landscape of hazard
and used next day, next year
for finches, the lilies
for Glen Canyon
and the morning silver greys
the painted birds at noon
walking through grit
repeating the songs
we're easily distracted from—

and we forget how the sun
and mountains pause
for last reflections, those tokens
taken from memory
of long dawns
the vast rouged sunsets
and time disappearing as light
illuminating all the forgettable places
those spaces soon to be forgotten.

II

On A Clear Day

Better watch the townsmen here
where the flat earth
has its partisans
and perpetual war, fervid advocates
while others promote
queer reenactments of battles
between history's good guys
and bad—better to play
pinochle or horseshoes
for under cover of a solstice
summers melt away
from coasts of the worn ordinary
sly and thoughtless
with last season's sachet
of lost causes, threadbare
herbal remedies
and the only age we have
walks with a hunch
to where everything continues
mindless, and things go on and on
down the road
in a forum of the public abyss
and no one is saying
—hey dude
let's hitch a ride.

Solvents of State

This is how a country comes apart
when it comes apart—
there will be no time-out
for the calm tedium of a garden
instead, a chair rocking slowly
at the railing
the age walking with a hunch
its anxieties projected on the low
clouds with minds given to the easy
and searching for the bottom
usually schooled on the cheap
with universal benefits for some
if illusory and brief. Though the end
may come on silent feet. Or with pitch-
forks and poles, and in all sincerity.

The Harsh History of Blue

Falling out of cosmic order
blue has leapt from sea to sky
to the pavonian infinite
where we lodge a brief
of hopeless grief
for our deeply impaired condition
—we have hardly noticed Armenian blue
has perished with the ice
of the Turkish avalanche
and Alexandria's blue vanished
long ago with Pharos and the Christians
in a February sky on fire
and Dresden blue once lay smashed
like the marriage porcelain
and only with effort restored
—yet from gardens in ruin
remembered periwinkles and hyacinths
still linger in untended borders
though blue arrived late on the rainbow
to color a kind of sadness
its multiple, troubled shades
wedged between the world's multiple bruises
and the unknown's paternal black.

Journey to a Funeral

Borrowed dust returns us to
wild places
hard to know
I try to squint through
a High Plains winter
at Monday's sheets
of ice laundered white
and folded and pressed
for December
and the dying huddled in their beds
the diffident spring times
and vandalizing rivers at flood
honeyed wheat waving
under the blue, a fly's rising
buzz lost to wide immensities
of the cemetery's sky
a landscape of hazard
and arrive at the shallow
terminus of a deep grave
the travelers on other roads
unknown, and unaware
like the random in the cast of dice
going to places, all the forgettable
places they never wanted to go
and to be forgotten again.

Last Dahlia

The final flower had neared its end
and we weeded it
along with the spurge
a succulent nemesis
leaving the old roses
and their threadbare accounts
aggrieved
and a green garden
ambushed
though everything
we had named
and held high hopes for once
was transplanted here
only to be forgotten again
on hazard's horizon

what we do next
our chairs rocking at the railing
leads to brown and orange dishes
on yellow cloth
a table set
for high winter and assisted living
an idle lunch
now breaking through the cosmic order
the day's distractions

and a cosmic indifference
tiny ants, a loud-closing garden gate
and a recent portrait
of the late sun's pose
for some lone bee
on its last flyby
to a still furled rose.

Mentioning the Unmentionable

—now we have something
you shouldn't talk about
and learning what is knowable
about longitudinal suffering
moving west to east
the telling of pain
its indeterminable time
and even in the short, reticent notes
where I write a name
—and finished just this morning
recapitulating better days
and already published to posterity
—though what the days will have to say
farther on
since pain nods to the future
and doesn't always leave an address
is harder to guess

Between Syllables and Sound

Threaded into the embedded
syllogisms of prayer
a music of hope
rises above the treachery
of self-referential tropes
with a dubious eye on the heavens
an already hazardous landscape
and the often misaligned stars—
the courier from wherever
is believed to arrive daily with repairs
in song and music
of the prayerful Hours—
even as we argue about
the wished-for but the not-to-have
and the arbitrarinesses
of those things that fail to be
or that could have been freely given
like rain
or hard to withhold like the wind.

Transparency

They live different lives
from you and me.
Far from the gardened suburbs
behind unclipped privet
the tense windows shuttered
interior lights turned down
they have found obscurity
in darkness.
Every offense taken
with the world
its recent, starker tone
the untranslated vocabularies
of the young
their privileged visuals
amplifying discordances and lost hope
moderated only a little
by the cabinet's small gin.
Older now, age walking with a hunch
the lonely dog and children gone
—suspect time holds them
on a tightened leash.

The movie of their daily
flickers faster
and things that should have
didn't work out.
A new world slipping into view
no longer speaking any language
they knew.

Orders of the Prodigal

Prized marbles
ordered and reordered
in phyla
their patterns clarified by
use, color, size—
once the envy of boys
still unused to cosmic order
chasing meadow stars
firefly flicker
and like Newton at the shore
along the worn coasts
of the ordinary
looking for a smoother pebble
the prettier shell
so that the one
necessary to replace the other
will fall into place

like happiness, love, the child
finding a mother
to end night's torments—
such tendered mercies
and small asymmetries
along life's scenic routes
through childhood
only partially hiding
the world's weird gravity
is sly compulsions
time's deep disorder.

The Lasting of What Matters

Where the words go
what was promised
what was intended
and always the evening's
inadequacy, words for love
used eagerly and casually
and Piaf singing
in the hoarse dusk, lanterns
waving every which way
a night sparrow on the wing
in one of the darkest nights
her words of love
coming back, worried
prayers in an addled hour
cabaret brasses and saxes
returning with soft warnings
then as comfort
a carnal evensong's chorus
of nostalgia
and you put down the knitting
put down the books

and you learn everything
loved is lost
to the anonymous air
once more
and all the forgettable places
forgotten again.

Composition of Absence

Those brief musical notes, plangeant tears of lutes. Evening again shaping morning thoughts about the old inviolates of family hatreds, their quotations from *le douceur de vivre*. A viola's taut mourning. The brooding exit of a woman losing the electric of her love. No nodding, no hellos in the hallway. In another room a complete consort dancing with a gavotte. In still another, a shadow waltzing among dancing lights. This is her lost history. And always the harangue of petitions to the nearby dark. Above a welter of glasses the woman lifts her young Traminer to an imperfect happiness. The sharpness of exile. In her carryon passages from aborted narratives. Unsorted nostalgias hidden among the regrets. The daughter who took her own life. A son—who married low. The pedals of a storm conceal unsolvable sums of past tonalities. Each time, the last note now in chance's random, still ahead. And the mercies, the mercies seem arbitrary.

III

Catching up with Time...

Taking our cue year after year
from leaves, the ice on creek water
and coasts of the worn ordinary
—and from summer, summer's long
largo and repetitive cicadian rhythms

we remembered a good life
and our youth—its very love
of love itself
and after shaking off anxiety
(is it the place or a time that I remember?)
anxiety lasting like
a child's summertime
worn like a dog's coat, now shook free

and tuned to each other's nerves
we now listen for the fragile amplitudes
the late afternoon sounds
like the mournful horns
of Mahler's gold
from a far autumnal space
footfalls on the porch
a screen door's slap-slam
gravel crunch of the Packard hearse and then—
shovels pinging at the skin of ice

a hand falls off the clock
that was losing time—funny, for years
we had thought of space as too small
and time
a habit that never stopped at all.

As for the Stars

early on you learn
to speak to them
like one who prays
while the first star
acknowledges wishes
now probably forgotten
yet you remember
the constancy of night skies
adrift in light
and what the stars seem
still to be saying
in the certitude of their clarity
—their threadbare points of view
new signs of cosmic indifference
in a landscape of hazard
until they fall out of place
following everything
of once bright promise

Half-past Four

soon a quarter moon
the day has already chosen
its winners and losers
...and now, later on
the road winds sharply into the night
headlands, a frayed woods
barely visible
that whistling figure
retreating just ahead
could be God (or someone else
someone who has had a hand in all of this)
—a spitting image
of course forbidden
and the remaining path is slight
with only fireflies for light
their lanterns
swinging every which way
the light beginning to disappear
with ships of whatever flag
like so much else in the vasty deep
of night's long night
and we wait breathless for sleep
to come up for air
past the palisades
past night's nervous radar
past the possibilities out much too far

Original Intent

We say America's peculiar
odor is not sanctity
and from our native deficits
politics will not save us.
Thomas More was woven
into his hair shirt
knowing well the smell
of burnt flesh and spilt blood
flesh of those he himself burnt
and at the scaffold bled.
Yet application of an extreme
must fall short every day
in the hesitant commonwealths
of nearly everywhere we know.
Tight zoning in the place we live
keeps the closest auto da fé
just beyond the settlers' means.
And the police's say.

Mood in a Minor Key

Your singing follows
the bird's grief
a bird in unmitigable pain
singing with a mother's loss
where you move along the winter
margins of your zippered space
looking for *what?*
until a door squeezes open
and your asking
in a shuttered voice
what could I do?
sunlight high in the iced branches
your hands extended
to reach phantom chords
but the note still sought
will have to wait.

How It Seems

The far end, that farthest end
where the options dwindle to
the suffering that awaits—suffering
often seen from an odd
angle of mind in pain—
a mother lost to time's fog
those forgotten in the prison at Shawnee
the dying huddled in their beds
lost travelers in a labyrinth
bodies broken, their spirit's bleakness
among the hard despairs—

places of mind, body, memory
forgettable and to be forgotten again
on a pathway of ache
running east out of time
time remembered now
for its enmity
and the age walking with a hunch
toward a bed
where one reaches comfort
lying still
knees fetal bent
hoping not to be noticed
after the numbness falls.

Cold Queries

While trying to explain
the disposition of
nearly everything asked
—like the death of children
those merciless withholdings from
the poor—
without turning to distance
and to the authority of the horizon
for answers

or looking up
similitudes with faith
in coincidences
but without boring the satisfied
and seeing how
the past, familiar and often pretty
collapses into cosmic indifference

like the gorgeous sound of rain
on the rust of corrugated tin
and how much happens or doesn't
that should or shouldn't
and with a narrow grace
lanterns waving every which way
to ships of whatever flag
we reach some unknowable
farther place.

Measure of Devastation: Part B

Who knows for sure
if death is not painful.
Some said *don't give all our*
Zyklon-B to the Jews.
The Führer won't let us suffer.
True, those were summers
known for mirrors and smoke.
Peeling from inland fogs
in a landscape of hazard's gaze
the rain-rotted barracks settled
just off their foundations.
The past buckled
like the road to Xanadu
from the military trucks.
What can it mean
when the light is so bad?
And this was the only time we had.

Latitudes of Grief

possibilities sometimes are not limitless.
The Cherokee finding Oklahoma
under the whip of force.
Pellucid Oklahoma, never the same again
turning to its dark interior
interior lights turned down
to brood on blood.
The Greeks rounded up
in Anatolia and sent to
someone else's home
to lament the malice of history.
The Armenians murdered long ago.
And the rest, the rest—
seabones washed up on sand.
And always the suffering witness
of the Jews to accuse. What more can be said
if distance is the sole temptation of space.
Space with its narrow wind
(or is it time having lost its mind?)

Horizons

Years, now, and the Far West spreading out before
you—like the desolate melodies of an infinite ranch.
Aspen leaves yellowed, Mormon wagons at a hitching
post. Yellowstone taking the veil from smog of guests
leaving. Ample guests. Bears angered out of their
acedias. A turquoise sky anticipating winter cloud
smoke. Coals falling lower and lower from Xmas fires
of fifty years and more. Along rural roads acres of dry
bones missing church again. Widowed tombs
arranging a rendezvous with the last day's endless.
Horizons stretched to the sadder parts of your own
city's limits. Ghosts tumbling out of the grumbling
darkness. North, South —East, West: each with wards
of preferred existential ruin. Doors, windows smashed.
A voice at two in the morning—from childhood.
Asking for water. For mother. Darkness mirroring
what the smallest desert intends. Will there be light—
light to rivet across the dawn? to keep the demons in
their shadows? Only certain silences remain of the
forgettable places to be forgotten again. The father of
the desert will say *there is light but your mother and
water will not return.* Though home is still a chronic
thought.

Visionary Gestures

Things seen and unseen
things the Buddha saw—
an enraged elephant in a trap
your hand swatting the fly—
always his cautious admonitions

yet how little the world
is changed for long
by solitary visions
of the heroic saints
those hoarse after deep silence

Teresa at her prayers
angels whispering at her ear
her chafed faculties
armored in graces
of scapular and cincture

in the middle of night, on the mind's
worn coasts of the ordinary
in prayers like syllogisms
knowing what to deny
what to affirm

—but our words are soon caught
in the insincerities of their tropes
though the holy separates
distractions from abstractions
like the storm from its wind.

Where Are the Memories...

where are the memories, the dead gone
missing, and the keys to the chiffonier?

on it there were two pictures
the son who didn't succeed, the son
allowed to disappear

on mapless roads, where did they go
hearing music across wide water
above the river's lap
and high water weirs

they wandered into shadowlands
near facsimiles between two distant stars

awaiting a final telling, seabones washed up
on the sand as two stories close the books
on the hush of their tracks

someone is talking, the age walking
with a hunch, someone is still erasing
what neither any longer can tell us
all the lights now turned down

IV

Personal Geometry

The High Plains at ground zero
meeting its sky behind windbreaks
a set for interplay of wanting
and needing present first in games
childhood plays
tapping a spoon
on highchair trays, demand
and want, animal need
more pabulum, more space
—all the outer spaces
waiting to be reined (the inner
an extra dimension, just in case)

and as a farmer
from one of the forgettable places
gleaning self-knowledge
with more acreage, a broader expanse
a bigger horizon for more light
when already as a child he parsed
happiness and unhappiness
and now comes to know

the degrees of difference
between what a child once thought
and the rectangular farms
their angles now pockets of small doubts
the industrial farming, soils depleting
a landscape of hazard
heavily mortgaged to the elements
(said when agency is obscure)
while the years
in their distracting interests
wait to be paid.

The House at Paint Creek

still stands
left behind on an eroded knoll.
The windows glinty, shutterless—
blinding in their threadbare
points of view. Porch pillars
diminished. Hills that rose
to meet imagination once
now fail expectation.
The road to a better world
passes by on the way to the past.
The stores have closed.
Jobs have moved to China
and the age limps along
carrying its own lunch.
The daily reverts to the mean
or worse, and the heartland
turns its back on excess.
With memory of any fine feeling
now trimmed to lean or less.

Petitioning the Horizon

In childhood I tagged along with my
father in the field backing up against
Murphy's borrowed woods.
There, owls lost their sky
and the land spread out
over buckshot and limestone.
Roads on the way to town
ran along fields, jogged level
and narrow-eyed through groves
shading ginseng and morels.
A landscape of hazard
if ever there was.
The town, eating into the land
once waited for trains to somewhere
—whistling through
pausing for a trunk
the tall-necked cans of cream
morning's mail
—and the town went back to sleep.
Road, woods, town and tracks
raced a distance with
the telegraph alongside
childhood and everyone's horizon.
And then disappeared in the press
of some undeclared need
for good.

Eclogue

Some of the animals that year
moseyed behind me past the orchard
like the cows from pasture
though the horses refused
and in the barnyard
ducks, the roosters and usually
the same two hens
even Frankie, the piglet
squealing at my heels
each of course had been suborned
by food and petting
when the dog blustering from the rear
fearing to miss something
food or walk or trip
and breaking rank raced
to the front scaring the chickens
but not the ducks or Frankie
and we repeated the march often
until the apples turned red
and fell into their unexpected fall
in the fugitive history of us all.

Meeting the Chimera Halfway

That summer of sudden storms went unspent
and black-eyed susans no longer mingled
with crawfish and the tangle of goldenrod
at Dry Fork Creek.

The creek overflowed.

And I still couldn't walk well
after the fall.
The woods moaned and sang
to the moon on tired wood all night long.

In grief I had to kill my dog.

There was ample leisure to read about
in the itinerant philosophies.
I already knew the Buddha
had once forbade the sea.

I learned to dread when the lights turned down.

And knew that water
even in a promiscuous climate
wants to follow a straight line
but rarely does.

None of this was enough.

What Things Know

Have they word from up ahead?
From the fallen barns along the river?
Oaken timbers once trying out
for the centuries, but from within
beams rotten in a wooden skin.
Time hiding from its own memory
the waste of its own making
in a rush to be forgotten.

Once past, does the past disappear?
A cosmic silence falling out
of a broken cosmic order
like running an errand in the wilderness
only to get lost like a seeker of morels
and then recede along a vanishing line
from a forgettable sight
to someplace forever.

Arrival at a Clearing

Looking for squirrel, Queen Anne's lace
whoever comes this way past the graves
may be in for a surprise

for once we were more than dust and bones
—the dead dancing elsewhere
with the dead while we sipped at our
drinks in the evening gardens of bygones

not that earth or this hillside is unclear
about intentions
—or foregone conclusions
hard to reach as one approaches near

what we are, what is, whose fault, all we felt
those things we might do over
merge here in the sift to silt.

The Domicile of Exile

We have been apart so long
it seems like willed exile.
Or like Ovid dispatched
for poor Roman behavior.
Where I was sent
(and why—hard to remember)
I hear the butterfly
luff and settle on a rose thistle.
Frost on the air tests the grit
of those who will stay.
Under ice to wherever
even now the creek trickles
on the way to some new place
if exile and water have a home
wanderer that water is.

The Nativity at Ames

Stars, stiff crunch of snow
—past a field of winter
wheat, past hazelnuts
my father picked each fall
at the narrow bridge
curving over the creek at Ames—
my parents and I are walking
in wartime to a country church
to see a giant Christmas tree
greeting us, the magi large-as-life
and alive in regalia of the East
(pointed out to me
as neighbors I don't recognize)
oranges, a banana
(gifts then winter exotic)
with nuts and candy
and returning past the hazelnuts
uprooted years after
our hands hand in hand
my father touching the night
he will later disappear into
my mother now alone at the gate
a sketch of us
as in another history of us
and the world shrugging its shoulders
years before I knew it.

Where Emptiness Settles

Some places I choose
to come back to
time has chosen
not to keep.
Stables, barn, the house itself
at Dry Fork Creek.
None of this erasure I foresaw
as I stand guessing
where everything stood
now razed.
Moss-edged, shingled sheds
sheltering tools
the chatty sparrows.
Wind chasing a grey light
whistles in the fields
of chastened space. Across late
winter, its taut meager farms
the winter wheat still green
in the forgettable places
to be forgotten again.

Canticle
for Early Morning

The bell rope rings
a raspy note on the toll
spreading out over cornfields
and spent phantoms of
a previous crop
the moonlit stalks in rows
now bent at the knees
frost heavy on roofs
air thick with softened muffle
of white, a music singing
with clarity of the chill
across the wintry fields
voices heard again
in the lashing tongue
of the bell, then vanishing
everything gone
inside except for the worn
façade of a fading moon
the presence full
somber and cold
a settling of cosmic indifference
over the land, leaving our space
alone, and old.

V

Trespassing on Time

We were high-minded
in the best sense, speaking
with inside voices
not wanting to be loud
about the trivial and petty—
we drove the broad county
never quite engaged
for fresh fruit, early corn
often stopping to look at
new clocks in the old shops
and after sensing time's *déjà vu*
turned back
to where we left off—

in increments finding
age's ignoble pains
the nation's perpetual
fondness for war
devious high speed trading
illicit pre-market gains
(the bounty set aside for the poor
— of course)

and a matinée newsreel
reading back to us canned tracks
of old catastrophes
until in the spirit of spite
middle management
wanting better news
turned up the light.

Sailing to the Moon: Tahiti 1947

for Clifford Ratz

War over—the long distances
remembered as pagan
norms with fewer boundaries
surely there was a grudge
against orderly Illinois farms

slipping into Papeete unseen
across the Sea of the Moon
with *Typee* in his knapsack
he had barely heard of Gauguin
the native women—the islands
he knew the islands
the Carolines, Marquesas
from wartime

a sour cherry again in fruit
when he left
there he had caught a bluejay
that would not sing
and turned it into a pet
he freed
as he was leaving, a pardon
he repeated

coming back just once
the young grown old
and roofs of the familiar and known
fallen in, he appeared
to have forgiven everyone.

After This Nothing Happened

Chief Plenty Coups
of the *Crow Nation*

After the Indian trails, the indirection
always the elusive cures
to ancient maladies we no longer name
—old talismans, the nervous hope
remain the gold standard—
rubbing of base metals against skin
tin bands, copper bracelets, lead
bangles for fortune, health
cures that may work
if you believe

and gold itself
still credible
its healing properties known
as in the goldwater cure
of the Doctor of Physic
sometimes as a therapeutic of mind
and a head shivered by a cold inland fog
or for the few, a ticket to time
and the strawberry fields

for the rest
generic antidotes that heal or not
—broken things of the heart
missing teddy bears
a mother's tears
the missing years
and all the forgettable places
steadying us for doubt
about the resolve of cosmic gravity
in a fast, unraveling universe

—so isn't this exactly what
the formularies get wrong
things the reasons can't explain
(Hume warned us
of being casual about the causal)
—we wonder at the inexplicable
confidence of the mockingbird
singing and hopeful, as if at prayer
and maybe knowing more
than us, still unaware.

Not Likely To Be the Last Word

Pigeons standing flocked together
their backs to a patented setting sun.
The poor still wait for some trickle
from the trickle-down.
And peoples of color
seldom do well here.
Though the pensioners
sense the odds—their age
in the crosshairs
of the heedless rich—
that this is the economy
their only time is up against.
Such is the oddity
the daily quiddity
while the birds fly toward oblivion
without further thought
and no word from farther on.
In the end don't we have to be surprised?

A Stiff, Straight-Necked Vase

"In the end it is just a white bottle." Morandi

It has avoided
the gluttony of an urn.
The Modigliani neck
springing from sour clay
under milkstar glaze
casts a narrow shadow
rising to severity
of the worn and ordinary
on an absolute scale.
It could hold a spray
of bitters. Or a candle
to the pitch black
of nothing's night
if fortune and the stars
fail to align just right.
This, then, we had best keep
to ourselves.

Drift of Delft's Blue and White

unnoticed, it idles here in its death
a single red rose
taking the delft out of blue
as a window's upper light reaches the table
at exactly twelve noon
where survival of things banal
trumps the tranquil
day, a celebrity-toned voice
running on and on
and rising against
the flower and vase
a rattling off of something
enduringly small
leather at Chieti
snorkeling off Aruba
the flags of whatever cruise
yet a brief sketch of us
the days always numbered
and, yes, the life unexamined

At Home on the Range

Under evening heat the land stretches to wake up. Hal
wheels his Peterbilt rig into Amarillo's low yellow
light in a landscape of hazard. Here horseflies fly
under radar. Only their buzz gives them away. And the
terrific thunk when they hit the truck. He has driven
from Bayonne, New Jersey, where cosmic order hides
from mean streets. Bayonne is not home. Tumbleweed
clings to the traffic light at Bell and Locust. A hoarse
wind spits sand. Home can never be just any place.
Surely not the repetitive Interstate. Or Ella Mae's at
the Arkansas truckstop. Grady the mutt hangs out in
the yard. A scruffy mynah says Heil Hal! when Hal
comes through the door, pulls up a stool at the
kitchen counter. The wife left years before. Son Jack
smiles from his oversize graduation picture. It used to
be on the TV before the widescreen. Jack never came
back from Iraq. So you deal with the hand dealt. Hal's
sister keeps house. In Amarillo they often do take-out.
At home most of the offenses against the senses are
repeatable. But isn't it here where things are you will
later miss?

Impulses in Counterpoint

what began early
nature's offhanded slights
of cosmic indifference
falling out of a cosmic order
and sending us to tears
returns loud with complaint
about all the lost preferments
of family, friendship, career
and then bewildered
we seek a mother again
from our infancy
her form leaning over us
and from her mercies
a touch changing
late morning tragedy
to carousel musics
and a sunny coast in pastels
until we feel
in the razor of a voice
those old rebuffs return
and after practicing regrets
learn to read and write
in briefer notes

Nearing Santa Fe

By twilight I want to believe
what is necessary to believe.
A landscape of hazard
and the wind about to blow
in a blight from a region of contraries
—the ash trees with their fungus
will lose their leaves in July.
Lodge guests at Sedona
a summer view (I imagine)
though I'm not near
enough to see. And somewhere
but not here, not now
there was a calamity, certainly
(or was it calamities?)
and all the lights went out.
An eclipse of the sun
and eventually of the sun's dependencies.
(Was it only cosmic indifference?)
In this evening's night, music plays
late hours in the canteen. We dance.
Though in the darkness I will have to keep
looking for lanterns waving every which way
and candles that spit at the dark.

Late Fall and a Round

Passing over, into
across and off
each other's radar
and approaching what
the unknown is like
lanterns waving

every which way
we stayed honest
and kind, growing
old, asking nothing
of each
the other could not give

and evening
exchanging a small rest-
lessness for rest
dangled before us
mottled enamel of the moon
displaying its grand calm

though shooting stars
dove into the dark
hidden fields
knowing what they know
like a night music
of still and cold

while we watched
from the world
taking us
past guttered candles
the icons in their intensity
to where we, too, will stare.

In Lost Pursuit

Caution followed her
through a landscape of hazard
after the confinement
and she walked out empty-handed
a survivor of her life
the geese honking over the pond
a radio tuning to old soaps
the fear
of unmasking never leaving her
someone at the door
the chair rocking at the railing
the phone ringing at an odd hour
letters without returns
surreptitious ways of
the hypothetical
asking her to explain
what she feared
and then at the door, fear again
when she had almost forgotten
and something in the wind rapping
someone with blame in hand
even after the pains she had taken.

Last Train from Blooming Glen

Snow flies at the street lights
covers old certainties of childhood
those threadbare points of view
(the best things in life are free
breakfast is good for you).
The dogs are barking
behind their fences and your father
whistles in the middle of a dark night
blinded by an inland fog.
You look for the station
to find a way out
but trains no longer run.
Someone says
they haven't for years. The tracks
nowhere to go and the depot
a bed and bath boutique.
Yet there's a conductor selling tickets
to late-life themes.
An organ plays a passacaglia
for everything lost
and all the forgettable places
to be forgotten again.

Still carrying all of your faults
in one bag, you want a booking—
probably on the coastal line.
Maybe near somewhere warm.
And something different and true.
Not too far from good schools.
Close to the necessary observances.
Possibly a view.

VI

Purposiveness without Purpose

Critique of Judgment
Immanuel Kant

The ghost of Homer
still sings in the attic
with most of your life
now in photographs.

You suspect when you reach there
—the there at there, if you ever do
you, with the purpose-driven life
the failures, its losses
still ringing in your ears—it won't be there.

And if it is—like contemporary cuisine, it will be
something hypothetical or metaphysical
a presentation on the bed of something.
Maybe something pureed.
Maybe beautiful. But probably not.

Just as you might have known
even the flowers of the middle kingdom
are plastic
and the gardens should be seen
at a distance or only at the margins.

Every journey from the heart
now travels without horizons.
And in later years the loss
is greater than anyone imagines.

Unfinished Business

The water table rising
all week long.
A flood restrained
only by palisades
urges itself on the plain.
Think of chance.
The unknown mind of God.
Then the boil of earth
the grass quivering
and a coffin surfacing
like a resurrection.
The life once suppressed
twitches into a freak flash
as if to make a dash to
the twilight border
where the dead
lord it over the living.
While the world
knowing all along
it has been made crooked
settles
on going round.

Singular Discernments

In what has become a scene
of the worn ordinary
diamonded pinkies flash their
glittery sunsets. And bottles of
$700 Sassicaia later
on the 4000 square foot deck
lights turned down
the girls and women molested
and the party over—
won't there be an invoice
for all of this?
Trees, golden maples in profusion
facing a violent season
first begin to shake
their leaves
although they stand their ground
all summer canopied as expected.
By winter they tremble naked.

Shorter Cadences

The small protest
of Indian Summer vanishes
on a heavier foot
than it entered on
                          and I hear rain
against the window
tapping out a staccato
and taking my hand
leading me toward the edge
of iron winter and away
from the dimmed humming
of summer measures
—our pleasures
in the dart and skip of colors
and the monarchs on their way
to Michoacan
—then the darker
nights turning longer than day
and an age now walking
with a hunch.

I wait until morning
as time drifts in
in place of the sun
interior lights turned down
hiding the open stealth of shadows
and what remains
of the shade hanging in folds
and time's cupped hand
waiting for change.

Very Likely in France

You still expect a path
out of the past to discover
what has long gone
missing. A mother, alone
and sitting on a sea wall.
Perhaps in France.
It must have been France.
Summer, likely.
And a day like any other.
A chair rocking at the railing.
Interior lights turned down.
She never returns.
Years will lose all
trace and then forget.
A lamp is brought in
to help you sleep.
It goes out.
And you grow up
knowing words
are insufficient even after
their flutter of excess
at everyone's loss.

Portrait in Chiaroscuro

If there will be any dialogue
some give and take

between a soldier's meager room
the French damp and a cigarette

and your eyes guarding
whatever secrets
and the body's entire
panoply of wiles

these—
memories will see
what the eyes never saw

a landscape of hazard
worn coasts of the ordinary
time's threadbare points of view

and this will matter less, later
when a woman's finger
on the camera shutter
fixes you on a bench in a peony garden
temple-walled, the tender-tended
morning Suzhou hot
and where you felt you were dying

still, the animal body yielding
nothing, not yet

but I wish I could bring myself to ask
if to die is to dissemble
about matter and soul

if after the boxwood parterre
a wild ride along some road
in your last delusions
a lost lane
of maple, river birch
and, quick, entering a hidden wilderness
with all the selected secrets

and listening to the incontinence
of an austere bell ringing
throughout the night from a hill
the stars' own incoherence
far beyond the bell of sky
and a river below in silver
flashing its light as you pass over

you find it is difficult to know
it is difficult to know for certain

what to reveal along the way
what effort to make or not

through indifference or diffidence
by omission or lie
by inference, what to conceal
and which distinctions are real

someone else will know the difference.

Regal Indigence

I was young yet
and watching my magic in mirrors
knew only my own pain
but half-knew what to expect
of those days of cumulus
collecting over water
and the coasts of the worn ordinary.
The importance of a life
as an idea we can't agree on
I never pursued. Though the absence
of something more, something needed
was never doubted.
I waited for an epiphany
maybe strobe lights and stars
(though the more scenic views
of the cosmic order were in decay)
and I joined in the applause
for a cargo of graces
thought to be on the way and already
in the shipping news, now read
daily, But I won't speak of the grand—
only of the plain sense of things
as Stevens said.

When Light Escapes Us

Everyone we knew
is here, and nothing has escaped our
notice, and in the long migration
no one seems left out

the dying huddled in their beds
their knees fetal bent
and later asking our names
—if we could only remember
there in the strawberry fields of forever

where the stars sink
and in a dark graveyard gather
beyond our knowing
and we ask the way in
looking for a way out

then is this a prison
or a reprieve, a second chance
and something different
a wall turning into a window

looking out onto familiar places
with familiar names like Cape Lookout
and yet places no longer quite familiar
the names, places blurring.

Remembering Transience

Now even death seems one of those
flash-by phantoms
whispering comforts and escape
in the being and becoming
of our days
though the gardens of empire
those special gardens
perpetual in conflict's care
blossom annually
in perennial white crosses, the stars
on the ashes of imperial ambitions
yet no garden or idea of garden
or idea itself
is remembered by death
the dying huddled in their beds
a sketch of us as in another history of us
to be forgotten again
in all the forgettable places.

Ventura Vespers

The sibilant hour gathered us
in the evenings. A balcony
potted with geraniums. Two chairs
and a table set with unmatched glasses
nearly mirrored a troubled cosmic order.
The long suffering
of the innocent, sick and the poor
in the divine economy
was never explored.
From an old landscape of hazard
we remembered our own shadowed love
a shadow life
and broken things of the heart.
We sat in the declining shade
of Lord Shiva saying the words
to the mantra we had learned.
His silent arguments
about purpose and focus in a material world
muffled an evening
now slightly deranged.
A balcony, our two chairs, a table.
The words we repeated to the wind.
Each time the stories slightly changed.
We listened for calm in the far beyond
and had to wait for a moon to shush the wind.

Weather in the East Comes from the West

Wind has words for things as they are.
Words on the wind thunder by
to where? to where even hard words go

—think of the random in chance
leaves twitching on the trees
the trees looking every which way
and what can they have been thinking
or whatever trees do
as the anxious brow of the West
mulls ideas
such as *it is what it is*

think of the unknowable mind of God
or some variant on this
since disorder hides
in the inner seams of an age
singing its discord
and walking with a hunch
the interior lights turned down
even as the east rises
almost above the limit of its limits
light riveting across the dawn

and then the sun
shuffling in from the back
and day now set in its ways
to enlighten a world
already rebuked by Tu Fu.

What seemed new
in new light now looks worn
like the coasts of the ordinary.
This will become the look of everything
at high noon
in all the forgettable places
soon to be forgotten again.

About the author

The Light off Cape Lookout is Robert Bense's ninth published book of poetry. He and Sonya Lyons live in Sacramento, California, and Waterloo, Illinois.

Belle Fontaine Editions
Robertbense.com